the Magic of GREATER VANCOUVER

BRITISH COLUMBIA, CANADA

A Photo Guide by
Philip Hersee

Published by
PHILIP HERSEE AND DON ATKINS
for
TOUCH THE MAGIC PUBLISHING INC.

Touch the magic

FOREWORD

"The beauty of Vancouver has inspired our work here."

U.S. President Clinton, April 1993

". . .Vancouver is the pick of Canada."

George Bernard Shaw, 1943

"Phil Hersee's photographs are among the very best in the world and we are a fortunate city indeed to have him portray Vancouver. It is a wonderful match of a talented artist and an incredibly diverse and beautiful subject ...."

Rick Antonson, Executive Director,
Greater Vancouver
Convention & Tourist
Marketing Association

TABLE OF CONTENTS

Every Top 30 destination has a **1** number that can be quickly referenced to the map both from the Quick Pick Listing or from the pages on which they appear. Other Greater Vancouver destinations shown in the book are referenced by the appropriate page number only.

OUR TOP 30 DESTINATIONS

1 Stanley Park

2 S.S. Beaver

3 Vancouver Aquarium

7 Gastown

8 Chinatown/Dr. Sun Yat-Sen Garden

9 Science World/Omnimax Theatre

13 U.B.C. Nitobe Memorial Gardens

14 Queen Elizabeth Park

15 Pacific National Exhibition

19 Grouse Mountain

20 Capilano Suspension Bridge

21 Horseshoe Bay

25 Reifel Bird Sanctuary

26 Fort Langley

27 Minter Gardens

We believe these thirty destinations highlight the magic of Greater Vancouver and its environs and provide visitors with an overview of the city's exceptional charm. Locations are easily referenced to the double-page map overleaf, and can be explored in a few hours, a few days or longer.

4 Canada Place

5 The Lookout! Harbour Centre

6 Vancouver Art Gallery

10 Granville Island Market

11 Vanier Park Museum Complex

12 Museum of Anthropology at U.B.C.

16 Simon Fraser University

17 Burnaby Heritage Museum

18 Lonsdale Quay

22 Royal Hudson

23 B.C. Museum of Mining

24 Whistler Resort

28 Steveston

29 New Westminster Quay

30 Gulf Islands/Victoria

USEFUL NUMBERS	
Arts Hotline:	684-ARTS (2787)
B.C. Environment (fishing & wildlife):	582-5200
Canada Customs Information:	666-0545
Canada Immigration Centre:	666-2171
Emergency:	911
Fisheries & Oceans:	666-3545
Interpreter Services:	684-2940
Lost & Found:	
B.C. Transit	682-7887
Police property room	665-2232
Road Report:	525-4997
Ski Information:	669-SNOW (7669)
Sportsline:	280-4400
Ticketmaster Arts InfoLine & Charge-by-phone:	280-3311
Weather report:	664-9010
Greater Vancouver Visitor & Convention Bureau:	683-2000

Please refer to Travel Information & Services on page 80, for more emergency, transportation and other useful advice.

DESTINATION MAP

"Dream-filled hills that swim into the sky
amid their everdrifting clouds of pearl and grey"

Pauline Johnson, First Nations author-poet

Greater Vancouver's poetic quality releases the imagination and captures the heart. From dawn until dusk and through every successive season, it's a magic sparked with the vitality of youth and mellowed with the glow of experience.

Since ancient times, the magic of this area has been honoured by the Haida, Coast Salish and Musqueam peoples. Their myths and legends still texture the city and their native culture prevails with distinctive art, giant totem poles, centuries-old burial trees and names that linger, as in a dream . . . Siwash Rock, Kanaka Creek, Capilano River, Semiahmoo Bay.

When Capt. George Vancouver surveyed the land in 1792, he spoke of it as "the most lovely country that can be imagined." His words became an invitation to fur traders and pioneering explorers. By the mid-nineteenth century, gold, coal and vast tracts of lumber were discovered and an early township was flourishing. Vancouver received its city charter in 1886 and a year later, when the Canadian Pacific Railway forged its way through the Rockies, the ramshackle community was linked to the rest of Canada. Growth was rapid.

Vancouver has been Canada's third-largest city since 1930. It has prospered with immigrants from across the country and around the world and is among the fastest-growing urban areas in North America.

Today, Vancouver is sophisticated and vibrant, in vogue and energetic. Downtown streets teem with people and there's a rich ethnic mix in the shops, restaurants and neighbourhoods. Where sawmills and fishpacking plants once stood, a metropolis of glass and steel has risen to become the western focus of the world's second largest country.

The youth of Vancouver's history is evident. Downtown is clean, safe and sparkling with fresh-faced virtue. Shiny new towers soar upwards, side by side with architecture that speaks of another century. Older buildings are cherished, not bulldozed. Façades are uplifted and masonry nurtured.

The skyline is one of the city's great treasures.

Many of the gleaming skyscrapers serve as corporate headquarters to the province's resource-based forestry, fishing and mining giants. But as these companies restructure their industries to the changing environment, their leadership roles are being assumed by entrepreneurial ventures in telecommunications, marine subsea vehicles, electronics, computer software, environmental and aerospace technology.

Tourism is Greater Vancouver's number one business, and activities for the visitor abound.

It is a shopper's mecca that ranks with the very best in the world, with designer name fashion in elegant stores, souvenirs, outdoor markets, galleries, museums and beautiful gardens. Over 3,500 restaurants offer cuisine from every corner of the globe, and accommodation ranges from three five-star hotels to the charm of intimate, European-style bed and breakfasts.

Of the 1.7 million residents who live in the Lower Mainland, more than three quarters of the work-force is in service industries including banking, insurance and real estate.

The area's robust performance is credited to its perfect coastal location – equidistant between Europe and the Pacific Rim, and only 30 miles north of the U.S. border. And Vancouver's designation as an international banking and financial centre is attractive to offshore investment. These monies, particularly from Japan and Hong Kong, are fuelling one of the strongest economies in Canada.

More than 3,000 foreign ships a year visit Vancouver's naturally deep harbour, including luxury cruise liners en route to the Alaskan glaciers. Port facilities are among the busiest in the world with 25 specialized terminals handling sixty-six million tonnes annually in coal, petroleum, forest products, grain and minerals.

Film and television production is also booming and pours $250 million each year into the economy. Nicknamed "Hollywood North," Greater Vancouver offers five film studios – one with the largest special-effects stage on the continent – and a pool of production talent to rival the world's best. When teamed with beautiful surroundings and magical backdrops, it's little wonder that Vancouver's film credits include *Cousins, Bird on a Wire* and *Look Who's Talking II;* that television series *The Commish, Wiseguy* and *MacGyver* have been shot on city streets, and that celebrities Sean Connery, Katharine Hepburn, Bob Hope, Sylvester Stallone and Tom Selleck have all called Vancouver 'home.'

More than a just city of great beauty, Vancouver offers a host of activities at destinations that are wonderfully accessible, whatever the mode of transport.

Vancouver's compact core makes walking a pleasure and the city's excellent integrated transportation system of busses, rapid transit and ferries quickly connects some sixteen cities and municipalities that make up the Greater Vancouver region. With an unlimited one-day pass, travelling becomes an inexpensive ticket to a variety of sightseeing delights. Taxis are plentiful and driving is easy.

Seaplanes, ferries and steam trains will take visitors a little further afield . . . to fly above alpine meadows, to cruise through the Gulf Island inlets, or to relax in hot water springs.

The region's mild marine climate is the envy of the rest of Canada, with comfortable summer temperatures that average 22 degrees celsius (72 degrees fahrenheit) and a winter thermometer level that rarely dips to freezing. And coastal rains are welcomed. They freshen the water, rinse the air of urban pollution and lavish the city's streets and boulevards with lush displays of colour. There are promiscuous croci and daffodils in February and a rainbow of azaleas in March. In April, over 60,000 cherry and plum blossoms soften the scenery with a hazy pink glow. Summer brings glorious technicolour and, come October, there's the brilliance of autumnal bronzes.

The West Coast lifestyle is shaped by sports and outdoor activities. Whatever the time of year, sheltered city plazas are filled with office workers enjoying their lunch breaks. Commuting cyclists weave in and out of traffic, joggers sprint along Stanley Park's 10km- (6 mile-) sea wall and para-gliders brace for flight off Grouse Mountain. And there's always someone fishing. Early spring breezes see sailboats – their spinnakers a blaze of colour – and windsurfers skimming across whitecaps among the anchored freighters. Skiing starts at first frost and ends only at the height of summer when attention turns to baseball diamonds, cricket wickets, golf and bowling greens.

Spectator sport is followed with gusto and is action-packed. B.C. Lions football roars beneath the air-supported dome of B.C. Place Stadium. The Vancouver Canucks celebrate twenty-plus years in the NHL with a new host arena. The Vancouver Canadians (Chicago White Sox's

Triple-A farm team), provide great family entertainment at Nat Bailey Stadium and there's plenty of opportunity for thoroughbred and harness racing, international soccer, golf and tennis tournaments. Annual events such as the International Dragon Boat Races in False Creek are becoming world renowned, and thousands enjoy the Abbotsford International Air Show, the Molson Indy Vancouver and the city's International Marathon.

Greater Vancouver's remarkable ethnic mosaic has enriched its cultural appetite for galleries, museums and theatre, inspiring performances that are flamboyant and innovative. The Symphony goes up the mountain. Grand opera is staged in a stadium. Ballet is danced in a mall. Shakespeare is performed on the beach and Broadway musicals are sung outside, under the stars. International touring companies with presentations such as *Les Miserables* and *Phantom of the Opera* play regularly to appreciative audiences and street performers, mimes and musicians brighten up many a downtown corner and transit station.

Throughout the year, the city stages festivals celebrating a lifestyle, a culture and an energy that is uniquely West Coast . . . from carol ships adorned with Christmas lights, which glide through the mid-winter darkness, to barbecued salmon at the beach beneath a canopy of exploding fireworks.

Vancouver's international flavour is mirrored in every facet of life. Authentic pockets of Europe and the Far East are open for everyone to explore and, with the cuisine of over 35 nationalities, dining is an epicurean affair. Japanese sushi bars compete with Indian curries. Thai spices rival Moroccan seasonings. Vietnamese spring rolls vie for attention with French patisseries. Little Italy on Commercial Drive has pasta on every corner and the Greek tavernas on West Broadway serve up belly dancing with souvlakia. And discovering Chinatown - the second largest in North America - is to be enveloped by the sights and scents of another country, with all the exotic flavours to match. It's a magic entirely unto itself.

Vancouver's natural splendour has been compared to the world's beautiful cities such as Hong Kong or Rio de Janeiro. But Vancouver's unique West Coast charm offers more. It has the sparkle of creativity, the vivacity of lifestyle and the sophistication of an international player. In all senses, Vancouver is out of the ordinary - with qualities than can only be described as magic.

STANLEY PARK

Brockton Point, Stanley Park
Kwakiutl and Haida totem poles now stand on what was once a pioneer cemetery.

Prospect Point, Stanley Park
In 1888, the S.S. Beaver, a Hudson Bay Company vessel and first steamship on this coast, was wrecked on the rocks below. A replica paddle wheeler of the same name, offers evening cruises to Indian Arm.

Lions Gate Bridge opened in 1938. It marks the entrance to Vancouver's inner harbour and is the half way point of the 10.5 km (6.5 mi.) seawall walk around Stanley Park. Look for nesting cormorants on the rockfaced cliff.

Outdoor artists of every palate – a flourishing Sunday tradition.

The First Narrows Military Reserve was set up as a precaution against an American invasion. And in 1886, when pioneers preserved the area as 1,000 acres of natural wilderness, they gave Vancouver a stunning oceanfront oasis in the heart of the city. Dedicated in 1888, by Canada's Governor-General Lord Stanley, it was a gift of infinite wisdom for generations to enjoy.

Today, there are wooded trails, secluded lakes, open playing fields and gorgeous gardens that continue to provide refuge from the hustle of urban life with a perimeter pathway of almost 10 km (six miles) that meanders along the fringe of the forest, at the edge of the sea.

Girl in a Wet Suit, inspired by the famous mermaid statue in Copenhagen Harbour.

The attractions within Stanley Park are numerous, and among the most popular is The Vancouver Public Aquarium, the largest in Canada. Over 6,000 marine animals from every watery corner of the world enjoy unique and spectacular settings from steamy Amazonian jungles to icy Arctic waters. Killer whales and belugas can be touched - almost - from expansive underwater windows. Many of the playful seals and otters are part of an extensive marine mammal rescue and rehabilitation programme that has cared for over 350 injured or orphaned animals over the past 30 years.

Children's Petting Zoo.

Miniature Train Ride.

Seasonal Gardens.

Pitch & Putt.

ENGLISH BAY

English Bay is for people-watching with front row seats to a kaleidoscope of flexing body builders, strolling grannies, beachside popcorn vendors and a stream of flamboyant characters from Vancouver's West End, the most densely populated square mile in North America.

This view looks West, towards Stanley Park.

CANADA PLACE

The magnificent white "sails" of Canada Place are one of Vancouver's most prominent landmarks, navigating three city blocks into the harbour like a sleek luxury liner. Once the Canada Pavilion at Expo '86, the complex now houses the Vancouver Trade & Convention Centre, the C.N. Imax Theatre, World Trade Centre, Vancouver Board of Trade, cruise ship facilities, a five-star hotel, restaurants, offices and shops.

SHOP

ROBSON STREET

Continental Robson Street brings Europe into the heart of Vancouver. Leading-edge fashion, sidewalk cafés, bistros, a lively public market and colourful buskers playing every conceivable instrument give "Robsonstrasse" a vibrant personality both day and night.

HARBOUR CENTRE

Getting oriented to Greater Vancouver is best done from The Lookout! – an observation deck 33 floors high atop Harbour Centre. A 360-degree view sweeps across the Lower Mainland from the mountains in the north to the valleys in the south and is coupled with a short, large-screen presentation on Vancouver and B.C. Plus, there's a wealth of information on current events and tours whether by foot, transit, coach, horse-drawn carriage, vintage car or paddle wheeler.

Vancouver's magic sunset lingers over the city centre and stretches to the western horizon that is Canada's gateway to the Pacific Rim.

DOWNTOWN VANCOUVER

Gleaming glass skyscrapers mirror heritage architecture. Downtown Vancouver has views from every angle, offering unique vignettes of Vancouver life, water, and mountains. Life is played out in tree-lined streets and intimate squares edged with seasonal colour.

Canadian Craft Museum, at Cathedral Place, is Canada's first national museum for both historical and contemporary crafts.

At the city's heart lies Robson Square, a people place of summer dancing on open plazas, the Vancouver Art Gallery, ice skating in winter and a lively conference centre which hosts a variety of exhibitions and seminars. The striking, glass-encased Provincial Law Courts are a few minutes walk to the south.

PLACED UPON
TO JULY 21

VANCOUVER ART GALLERY

Vancouver's heritage courthouse, built in 1911, was transformed into the Vancouver Art Gallery in 1983, completing the Robson Square complex. The architect, Francis Rattenbury, also designed the Empress Hotel and legislative buildings in Victoria.

The old courthouse entrance facing Robson Street is Vancouver's unofficial speakers' corner. Its steps are often covered in bicycle couriers taking a cappuccino break and has been affectionately nicknamed "Biker's Beach."

GETTING AROUND

Getting around Vancouver is fast and easy. Skytrain - an elevated advanced light rapid transit system - glides over the suburbs between the waterfront and New Westminster ("the Royal City" and first provincial capital) in just 28 minutes.

Twin-hulled catamarans called Seabusses shuttle foot passengers back and forth across the harbour to Lonsdale Quay and North Vancouver, while tiny electric ferries scoot across the inlet between Granville Island, English Bay and fashionable False Creek. Vancouver also has the largest fleet of busses in North America.

See page 80 for detailed Travelling Information & Services.

160 Vancouver
9003

GASTOWN

Gastown, restored with distinctive Victorian architecture, antique gaslights and cobblestone streets, reflects Vancouver's origins . . . both before and after it was burned to the ground in 1886! Gastown runs east of Canada Place along Vancouver's harbour and is peppered with historical references such as Gaoler's Mews, Blood Alley and a statue of the area's loquacious founding father, "Gassy" Jack Deighton, who ran a saloon here in 1867.

Turn-of-the-century warehouses have been superbly renovated into galleries, intriguing stores and restaurants. The world's first steam clock, that sounds the Westminster chimes, is powered by an underground steam system used to heat neighbouring buildings.

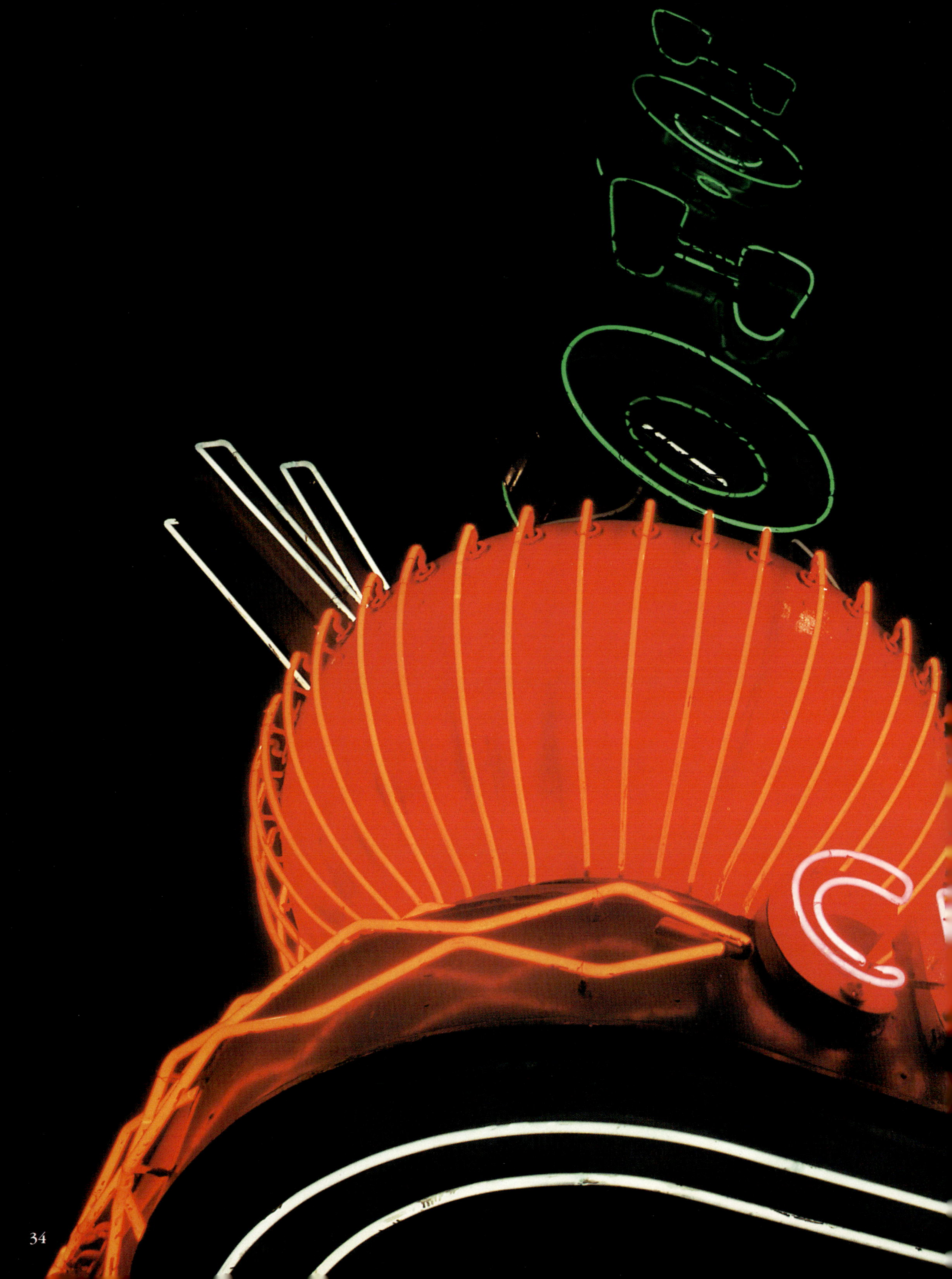

CHINATOWN

To discover Chinatown is to be suddenly engulfed with the tastes, sounds and fragrances of another culture. Streets bustle with colour and commerce, including Chinatown's own newspapers and distinctive street signs. Telephone booths are topped with pagoda tiles. Curious foodstuffs spill onto the sidewalks. Apothecaries sell ancient and exotic remedies of dried lizard skin and ground rhinoceros bone.

The Dr. Sun Yat-Sen Garden lies amid this chaotic fervour as a walled oasis of tranquillity. Named for the founder of the first Chinese Republic, it is the only classical Chinese garden outside of China and has been fashioned in Ming Dynasty style. Artisans from Suzhou used only traditional tools and techniques in its construction, and every pebble has been placed with painstaking awareness of its harmony with the environment.

The Chinese are Vancouver's oldest and largest ethnic group, who first came to the city in 1858 to join the Fraser Valley gold rush. Later, they worked in large numbers on the Canadian Pacific Railway or were contracted to the region's many fish canneries.

The Asian influence is seen in much of Vancouver's way of life. In schools, English is a second language of 40 percent of children. In business, almost half of the exports are to the Pacific Rim and in property, the most ambitious developments are being financed by monies from the Far East.

Dining in Chinatown is a voyage of revelation beyond simple fortune cookies. Nowhere is the journey more fulfilled than at a Dim Sum where small selections of food are continuously served from roving trollies, providing plenty of opportunity to try different dishes. Dim Sum means "to touch the heart" . . . and Chinatown is guaranteed to do just that!

Chinese New Year's Day Parade.

Dr. Sun Yat-Sen Garden.

Queen Elizabeth Park sits on Little Mountain, the highest point in Vancouver. Early morning visitors often see the slow and floating movements of Tai Chi masters silently welcoming in the day.

Science World and The Omnimax Theatre.
Visitors can touch a tornado and other imaginative hands-on displays, or be put in the centre of images magnified 75,000 times their original size and projected onto a 27-metre domed screen.

Pacific Central Station, across from Science World, is the western terminus for coaches and trains travelling to Banff, Jasper and across the country.

FALSE CREEK AND GRANVILLE ISLAND

Surrounded by marinas and enriched by views, Granville Island epitomizes the West Coast, outdoorsy lifestyle. Day and night, it's a thriving warren of shops, artists' studios, restaurants, theatres, nightclubs and galleries. Vancouverites flock to the rambling farmer's market, perched on the water's edge, to shop for freshly-picked produce, seafood straight off the boats, gourmet meats, bagels and handmade fudge. There's even an island brewery.

Once an industrial wasteland, there's still a sizable cement plant and blacksmithing shop operating amidst this creative mélange. There's a holiday feeling that prevails all year long and, as one of North America's most successful urban redevelopments, it has served as a blueprint for similar projects across the continent.

bridges
bridges
bridges

KITSILANO

As with many neighbourhoods, Kitsilano's name is derived from a Squamish Indian who settled in Stanley Park in 1860.

The Kitsilano neighbourhood is trendy and always full of activity. Smart new condominiums are wedged between older, character homes and lend an eclectic energy to the streets where alternative lifestyles and clusters of colourful shops still hint of the area's "hippie-haven" days.

People gatherings proliferate whether for great jazz or for children's festivities. In summer, Kits Pool provides heated salt-water fun and on balmy clear nights, Kitsilano Showboat stages a potluck of comedy, swing bands and dancing.

On the waterfront, millionaires' homes follow one another along Vancouver's "Golden Mile," quietly evoking the styles of the "establishment" that can be seen nearby, in the mansions of elegant Shaughnessy. Built in 1910, Glenbrae House is one of Shaughnessy's most spectacular residences and was once dubbed Mae West House for the two massive, round turrets that adorn its roofline!

The Canuck Place
formerly the Glenbrae house.

Kits Pool.

Kitsilano Showboat.

FIRST NATIONS PEOPLE gathering at Vanier Park.

VANCOUVER MUSEUM AND PLANETARIUM COMPLEX

The Vancouver Museum and Planetarium complex near Kitsilano Beach will enrich the mind with fascinating displays and activities. There are trips to the cosmos at the H.R. MacMillan Planetarium and to the stars at the Gordon Southam Observatory. Enjoy a journey back through time at the City of Vancouver Archives and the Vancouver Museum. And at the Maritime Museum, board the St. Roch, the first vessel to traverse the Northwest Passage both ways. Or, attend any number of free lectures that share the wonders of our maritime heritage to as far north as the Queen Charlotte Islands and beyond.

The distinctive conical roof of the museum and planetarium is patterned after the woven cedar bark hats once worn by the Northwest Coast Indians. In Indian legend, the crab is believed to guard the harbour and has inspired a giant stainless steel sculpture outside the building.

Vancouver Museum.

Maritime Museum.

Captain Vancouver.

UNIVERSITY OF BRITISH COLUMBIA

Founded in 1908, The University of British Columbia is a township in itself with live theatre, concert recitals, extensive libraries, resources, medical and athletic facilities as well as over 30,000 full-time students.

Discover one of the world's most impressive collections of First Nations art at the Museum of Anthropology at UBC; enjoy the solitude of authentic, classical Japanese gardens and stroll through a living museum of plants from around the globe at UBC's Botanical Gardens, established in 1916.

Located on the westernmost peninsula, UBC campus is separated from the city by a vast wilderness area, Pacific

UBC Nitobe Memorial Gardens.

The Clock Tower, UBC campus.

Spirit Park. Forested trails crisscross through 17 species of indigenous plant life, including cloudberry, a remnant of the last Ice Age 11,000 years ago. Narrow strips of the original 500-year-old forest can still be seen on the southern cliffs overlooking the Fraser River.

Museum of Anthropology at UBC.

Botanical Gardens, UBC.

Wreck Beach at the foot of "Trail Six" is for naturalists and nudists.

Jericho Beach over 3.2 km (2 miles) of sandy shore.

Spanish Banks is where Spanish explorer Lieutenant Narvaez first dropped anchor in 1791, a year before Captain Vancouver arrived. Hence the beach's name.

The quiet stretch of well-groomed sands and parkland from Jericho to Spanish Banks was once owned by The Department of National Defence. The Vancouver International Hostel is a former Royal Canadian Air Force barracks.

Kitsilano Beach is a mecca for fashion-conscious sunworshippers.

The Bloedel Conservatory at the top of the mountain is a 20-metre high triodetic dome consisting of 1490 plexiglass bubbles. It contains 500 species of plants and 120 free-flying tropical birds.

QUEEN ELIZABETH PARK

The abandoned rock quarries of Queen Elizabeth Park have been transformed into huge sunken rock gardens with ponds and waterfalls at every level.

PACIFIC NATIONAL EXHIBITION

Family fun, pink clouds of spun sugar and toffee apples describe Playland and the Pacific National Exhibition. Day or night, amusement rides mix with popcorn, agricultural displays with equestrian events, and pageants with parades, including the world-famous Royal Canadian Mounted Police Musical Ride. The PNE has been a wonderful Vancouver tradition since 1910 and is among the largest fairs in North America.

Burnaby Village Museum is an experience to savour. Costumed in the style of British Columbia's pioneer settlers, villagers tend their stores, their schools and their antique printing presses. Visitors can attend church, participate in classes or buy curative snake oils from the drugstore!

Vancouver by night - looking west.

BURNABY

Riding the waves of Canada's gold medal success in the 1992 Olympics and inspired by the performance of Silken Lauman, rowing is one of Canada's foremost sports. There are over 5,000 competitive rowers in Canada, and rowing has gained a strong foothold in high schools and universities alike. Burnaby Lake is one of the Olympic team's training spots in the west.

The award-winning architecture of Simon Fraser University on Burnaby Mountain was built in 1965 by Arthur Erickson who also won recognition for the glass-enclosed Law Courts at Robson Square and the Museum of Anthropology at UBC.

Secluded Deep Cove Village at the entrance to Indian Arm.

Mount Seymour – for hiking, skiing and sightseeing in a demonstration forest that sits at the foot of an ancient glacier-carved valley.

NORTH VANCOUVER

The two prominent peaks of the North Shore mountains, looming 1770 metres (5,800 feet) over the city, were once called Twin Sisters before early pioneers linked their likeness to the Lions at the foot of Nelson's Column in Trafalgar Square. Today, they are known as "The Lions."

Lonsdale Quay Market - a colourful indoor market of produce, boutiques and restaurants.

diet

GROUSE MOUNTAIN

Only fifteen minutes' drive from downtown and 1100 metres (3,600 ft) into the sky, Grouse Mountain is a year-round resort that offers hiking and horseback riding, picnics and logging shows, sleigh rides and skiing, restaurants and movies . . . and magical views of the entire Lower Mainland.

The Capilano Suspension Bridge was once called "Laughing Bridge" by the First Nations People and is one of Greater Vancouver's oldest family attractions. It crosses 150 metres (450 ft) of canyon over the swirling river rapids 80 metres (230 ft) below to pleasant parkland and trails on the other side.

The Capilano Salmon Hatchery nurtures about two million salmon eggs a year, and fishes in various stages of growth are visible through glass-fronted holding tanks. In spawning season, fish leap ladders into the hatchery, and are also abundant throughout the Capilano River as they make their arduous journey home.

WEST VANCOUVER

In early years, fish canning was the only real industry of West Vancouver, a modest tent and cottage hamlet. In the 1930s, the Guinness family of Britain bought 1700 hectares for $75,000 and carved out the Capilano Golf and Country Club and the British Pacific Properties, known today as The Properties. They are valued among the city's primest real estate and West Vancouverites enjoy the highest average annual income in Canada.

West Vancouver has retained a quintessential English look and has blended its hedgerows and perennial gardens with landscapes that touch the water. It even has its own doggy beach!

Enjoying Cypress Mountain. Look for the trail up to the Lions' peaks.

More than 200 cruise ships visit Vancouver each year to sail the Inside Passage to Alaska and are best viewed from West Vancouver's seawall at Ambleside and Dundarave.

Horseshoe Bay is the terminal for ferries to Nanaimo and the Sunshine Coast, where plenty of charters for fishing or cruising are available. Sailings to Victoria and the Gulf Islands depart from Tsawassen, an hour's drive south of Vancouver.

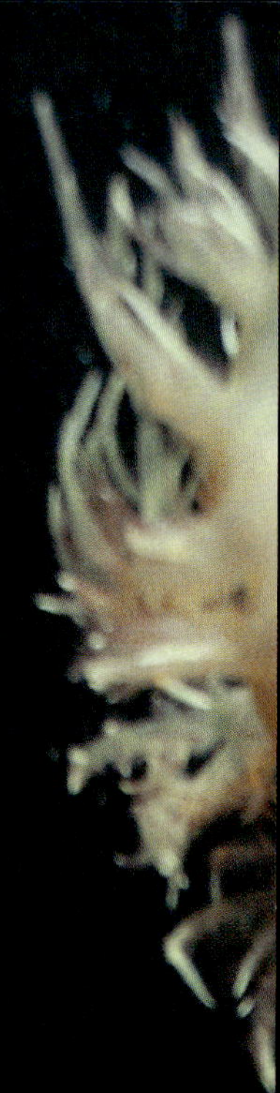

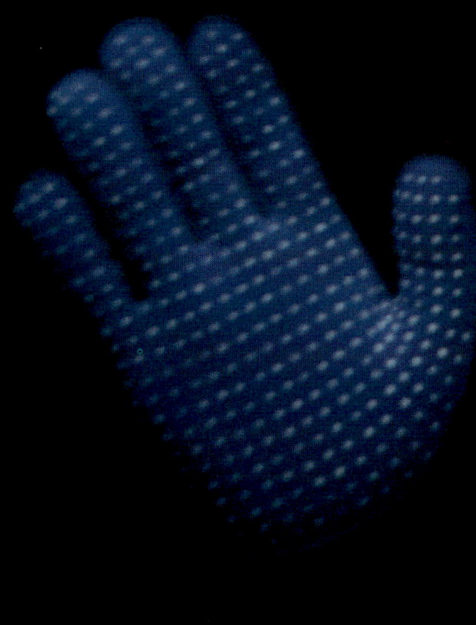

Lighthouse Park – a picturesque peninsula.

Howe Sound's steep-sided inlets and dramatic fiords show evidence of glacial activity, and the area is a diver's delight.

There's an incredible range of marine life in British Columbia waters with over 325 varieties of fish and almost 200 species of other watery wildlife that includes sponges, corals, abalone, prawns, anemones, wolf eels and the largest octopus species in the world. Whytecliff Park has an underwater reserve where marine life is protected.

HOWE SOUND

Describing Howe Sound in 1791, Capt. George Vancouver remarked:
". . . a solemn inland sea, studded with beautiful forest-clad islands, covered with towering trees whose branches at high tide are lapped by clear waters teeming with fish."

In the early 1930s, Britannia Beach was the British Empire's largest producer of copper and it now operates as the B.C. Museum of Mining, with underground tours on electric trains and panning for gold! Traditional tea shops are hidden treasures in many of the old, wooden homesteads and make an ideal break on the scenic two-hour drive up the coast. Whistler Mountain and neighbouring Blackcomb Mountain have become a full-fledged, four-season resort in a spectacular alpine setting. World-class skiing (Whistler is the nearest ski destination to Japan) and Arnold Palmer-designed golf greens are only two reasons to discover the mountains – and cosmopolitan Whistler Village offers many more.

Whistler Mountain.

B.C. Museum of Mining.

The Royal Hudson.

FRASER RIVER DELTA

To the south, beyond the modern metropolis of Vancouver, are the bountiful soils of the Fraser delta flatlands. Most of the area rises no more than two metres above sea level and since the 1860s, settlers hand-built dykes and drainage systems to ward off the Fraser River and the sea. Richmond is known as the Garden City and is both the blueberry capital of B.C. and the cranberry capital of North America. Picnic areas and U-pick fruit and vegetable farms abound.

Along the flats is the Reifel Bird Sanctuary, with Canada's densest concentration of over 250 species of wintering waterfowl and migrating shore birds.

On the opposite banks of the Fraser River stand some of the ancestral lands of the Musqueam Indians who built magnificent cedar longhouses, some as long as four city blocks. Today, they are among the province's richest landowners, and Southlands is a unique green corner of the city. Once the site of Vancouver's first farm, it has retained an open and pastoral atmosphere with horse corrals, barns and stables on every street.

Reifel Bird Sanctuary.

Minter Gardens.

Crazy Canoe Race, Chilliwack.

Fort Langley.

THE FRASER VALLEY

Communities in the Fraser Valley are among the fastest-growing suburbs in the Lower Mainland. The Fraser River, named for explorer Simon Fraser, is still one of the most abundant salmon rivers in the world, and has long made the valley lush, green and the bountiful breadbasket of the Lower Mainland.

Steveston is the oldest surviving community in the Lower Mainland and in its heyday, Steveston harbour was the busiest port in the world.

From the turn of the century, its history blended together the cultures of First Nations People, Japanese and Chinese labourers who worked in the fish canneries every summer. They spoke Chinook, a hybrid of English, French and their own languages, and with them, came a rough-and-tumble lifestyle that included gambling, opium-smoking and prostitution.

Steveston is a picturesque, historic site and still a place for working fisher folk. Visitors delight in buying their catch off the boats and strolling the promenade with its shops, cafés and galleries.

New Westminster Quay. Enjoy the busy public market and riverfront boardwalk that leads to a floating maritime museum, the Samson V paddle wheeler.

White Rock Pier. Five miles from the U.S. border, Indian legend says that White Rock was tossed onto the beach by a powerful sea god. Its dry climate has made the resort a celebrated holiday haven since the early 1930s, and fishing and crabbing are still popular pursuits from the 500 metre (1,500 ft.) long pier.

Vancouver Playhouse, Queen Elizabeth Theatre.

THEATRE ARTS

All the city's a stage with performances that range from international touring productions to telethons, ballets and operas. The Queen Elizabeth Theatre has two stages, the smaller of which is home base for The Vancouver Playhouse, a talented, regional theatre company and school.

Between "road trips" The Vancouver Symphony plays in The Orpheum Theatre – a beautiful facility, restored to its 1920s grandeur and highlighted by a 1,000-bulb crystal chandelier, gilt ornamental plasterwork and the original Wurlitzer organ.

Vancouver Symphony "on the road", bringing music to the community.

The du Maurier International Jazz Festival.

"Phantom of the Opera," Queen Elizabeth Theatre.

New Westminster, Hyack Festival.

A symphony of summer fireworks Vancouver Sea Festival.

FESTIVALS

Come rain or shine, communities are always vigorously staging fêtes and festivals, parades and processions, ceremonies, salutes and fanfares. Squamish has its Logging Days; Abbotsford its air show, the third largest in the world; Cloverdale its rodeo; Langley its Heritage Brigade and the Fraser Valley its agricultural fairs.

Whether it's ornate Chinese dragons undulating in their New Year's dance or the hundreds of hardy souls who brave The Polar Bear Swim on New Year's Day, celebrations like these are traditions that are cherished and shared throughout the year.

Asian Festival.

Folk Music Festival, Jericho Beach.

Children's Festival, Vanier Park.

Sea Festival, English Bay.

Vancouver International Dragon Boat Festival.

Squamish Logging Days.

Molson Indy Vancouver at Pacific Place.

Thoroughbred racing at Exhibition Park.

Vancouver Canucks.

B.C. Lions.

Sailing is a major part of the Vancouver lifestyle. With over 5,000 miles of sheltered waters at the city's doorstep, one in four families own a boat.

Canada Place, visitors becoming friends.

TRAVELLING INFORMATION & SERVICES

GOODS & SERVICES TAX

Foreign visitors can obtain a rebate on purchases and accommodation costs in excess of $100. For information, call toll-free: 1-800-463-6737. A non-refundable provincial sales tax is also charged on most goods and services.

EMERGENCY SERVICES

Fire, Police, Ambulance: 911, or dial "0" for operator

Marine/aircraft distress: 666-4302

Crime reports: 665-3321

Dentist referral: College of Dental Surgeons of B.C.: 736-3621

Doctor referral: College of Physicians & Surgeons of B.C.: 733-7758

Emotional Crisis Centre: 733-4111

Hospitals:

Burnaby General Hospital, 3935 Kincaid; Burnaby; 434-4211

Children's Hospital, 4480 Oak St., Vancouver; 875-2345

Lions Gate Hospital, 231 East 15th St., North Vancouver; 988-3131

Royal Columbian Hospital, 330 E. Columbia, New Westminster; 520-4253

St. Paul's Hospital, 1081 Burrard St., (downtown) Vancouver; 682-2344

Vancouver General Hospital, 855 West 12th Ave.; 875-4111

Poison Control Centre: 682-5050 or 682-2344 (local 2126)

Tourist Alert: the RCMP attempts to contact travellers with urgent messages via information centres, provincial campgrounds, newspapers, television and radio. Call 264-3111

Veterinarian: B.C. Veterinary Medical Association 266-3441 or Animal Emergency Clinic 734-5104

LIQUOR STORES & SERVICES

Liquor, wine and beer are sold only at government stores.
In British Columbia, the minimum age to purchase or consume alcohol is 19.
Liquor stores are closed Sundays.

LATE NIGHT PHARMACY (24 hrs)

Shoppers Drug Mart, 1125 Davie St., Vancouver; 669-2424

MOTOR VEHICLES

Seatbelts are compulsory in BC, motorcyclists must wear helmets and infant restraint systems must secure children under five years old. If involved in an accident with a BC licensed and registered vehicle, call: 520-8222 (Vancouver)

The BCAA offers 24-hour emergency road service to members of all auto clubs: 293-2222
To reclaim vehicles towed from the street, call: 251-1255
and from a private lot: 685-8181

METRIC SYSTEM

Canada uses the International Metric System for measures and weights. Highway distances are measured in kilometres. Gasoline in litres; temperature in Celsius.

POSTAL SERVICES

Many retail outlets, drugstores and 7-11 24-hour convenience corner stores offer postal outlets for consumer items such as stamps and basic mailing services. The main, full service, postal station is located at 349 West Georgia St.; 662-5725
Recorded rate information: 662-7222

SERVICE CHARGES

As service charges are not usually added to a bill, a general tip of 15% of the total amount is suggested to servers, hairdressers, taxi drivers, etc. Bellhops and doormen at hotels and airports should be given about $1 per item of luggage.

SERVICES FOR THE PHYSICALLY CHALLENGED

For information and a booklet entitled *Accessibility Awareness Vancouver Guide,* contact the B.C. Coalition of People with Disabilities, 204-456 West Broadway, Vancouver V5Y 1R3; 875-0188

TRANSPORTATION

Airport Express, known as the Hustle Bus, runs between Vancouver International Airport and downtown hotels: 273-9023

B.C. Ferries sail to Vancouver Island, the Gulf Islands and the Sunshine Coast.
Recorded schedules: 277-0277
information & reservations: 669-1211

B.C. Rail provides passenger services on the Royal Hudson to Squamish and the Cariboo Dayliner to Whistler and other northern provincial destinations: 631-3500

B.C. Transit operates throughout Greater Vancouver. Bus routes connect with SeaBus ferries and with SkyTrain: 261-5100
The blue West Vancouver Transit busses connect downtown with the B.C. Ferries terminal in Horseshoe Bay: 985-7777
For physically challenged persons, contact HandyDart Custom Transit Service: 264-5000 (ext. 5101)

False Creek ferries commute between Granville Island, south foot of Hornby Street and the Aquatic Centre on Beach Avenue. Call: 689-5858 or 684-7781

Helijet Airways flies helicopter services to Victoria's harbour and to Whistler. Reservations: 273-1414

Pacific Central Station, 1150 Station Street, is terminus for Pacific Coach Lines to Victoria: 662-8074
Maverick Coach Lines to Whistler, Nanaimo and the Sunshine Coast: 662-8051
Cascade Charter Service into the Fraser Valley: 662-7953
Greyhound Lines across North America: 662-3222
Rocky Mountaineer Railtours through the Rockies to Banff and Jasper: 984-3315 or toll free: 1-800-665-7245
For VIA Rail, call toll-free: 1-800-561-8630

Quick Shuttle runs from downtown Vancouver to Seattle city centre and SeaTac Airport: 244-3744 (toll free: 1-800-665-2122)

TALKING YELLOW PAGES

For up to date information on city news, activity, business and entertainment: 299-9000

TOURIST INFORMATION SERVICES

Tourism Vancouver provides advice and reservations on hotels,bed & breakfasts, transportation and tours throughout Greater Vancouver and beyond.

Contact or visit: Travel InfoCentre, Plaza Level, Waterfront Centre
200 Burrard Street, Vancouver, V6C 3L6
Information: 683-2000
Reservations: 683-2772